HOMAGE
POEMS IN THE VOICES OF THE
WESTERN CANON

Mark Brodeur

TATE PUBLISHING, LLC

Published in the United States of America

by Tate Publishing, LLC

127 East Trade Center Terrace

Mustang, OK 73064

(888) 361-9473

Grateful acknowledgment is made to the following for permission to quote excerpts from previously published materials: Samuel Taylor Coleridge, quote from lines 91-100 of The Picture; or, the Lover's Resolution, reprinted in Complete Poetical Works - The Complete Poetical Works of Samuel Taylor Coleridge, edited by E.H. Coleridge, Oxford, 1912, 1975 (quoted lines in italics); Walter de la Mare, Collected Poems, Henry Holt and Company, N.Y., 1941 (quoted lines in italics); Fyodor Dostoevsky, The Brothers Karamazov, translated by Constance Garnett, Penguin USA 1980 (quoted lines in italics); Arthur Schopenhauer, The World as Will and Representation, translated by E.F.J. Payne, Dover Publications, 1969 (quoted lines in italics); William James, July 11, 1885 letter to Catherine Walsh, reprinted in The Correspondence of William James, v. 6, 1885-1889, edited by Ignas K. Skrupskelis and Elizabeth M. Bradley, Univ. of Virginia Press, Charlottesville, 1988 (used as a source for the final three stanzas in James Grieving on Monadnoc).

ISBN: 1-5988630-1-0

To my Dutch grandmother Lottie, whose artwork graces the cover of this book and whose love of literature, philosophy and life inspires its contents

ACKNOWLEDGMENTS

While writing this book, I was thankful for the support of my family, my wife Bethany and children Brittany, Matthew and Jacob, as well as my parents Lester and Kate, brother David, sister Jennifer, and close family members Peggy, Pansy, Donald and Lottie. In addition, during the development of this manuscript, some of my closest friends were my best critics, especially Roland and Janet Leon, Jon Moothart, Gary Sarles, Shirley Smith, Tyler Fletcher, Luke Bilberry, the Muckleroy family and Donald Rowley. Last, I owe a special debt of gratitude to my patient and talented editor, Rachel Sliger.

TABLE OF CONTENTS

THE PHILOSOPHERS

A POEM IN PREFACE

If I were with you
    when you opened
        these pages,
            I would speak to you

and I would stop you
    from reading the poems
        before I told you the stories,
            as a parent would

when explaining
    his children to the world;
        but I am not,
            not with you,

so I will not
    be able to show
        how each of these
            is really a person,

and I will not
    be able to explain
        how each was born
            and came to be.

But if I were,
    were with you,
        I'd tell the way
            I began each person

by reading
   his works
      and biographies
      and criticisms,

letting that person
   arise himself
      or herself, then appear
         before me and begin to speak.

I would tell you
   how I waited,
      waited for each to be born
      from one sole image,

something each had lived
   or said, and how
      I let them grow up
      around those images;

I would tell you
   how I encountered these greats
      when they began to speak
      and how I dressed them,

dressed them in their own metrics,
   but how some asked to be
      freed, how Aristophanes
      was the first begging

to speak in free voice but
   how Tennyson would not allow
      himself to be taken out of
      the meter and rhyming of his time.

And you should not be
    surprised we've met this way;
        should not for we are
            eye to eye now, you and me.

Do you believe
    that I have asked
        all the greats back here
            to describe the soul? You should.

Can you imagine
    that the greats wanted
        to do this soul mapping
            when called back? You should.

Is it possible
    that their voices can be
        spoken again in this modern way,
            possible they had this left to say?

It is,
    is possible,
        and it is true—
            so listen as they speak to you.

THE WRITERS

PART ONE

The Greeks say the soul is made of light and darkness . . .

HOMER AND HIS TRIBE

Hear me, a speaker
who'll not read or write,
and trust me as one
who sees humanity,
but don't praise me,
listener of a future race,

for I describe
our own forgotten place,
that land where powers
fought and we were slain,
a time from which our
lesser selves remain.

High over the wandering
hosts we soared there,
above the lives of man,
and entered ancient spirits,
the gods at war, to be
their embodied flames.

See us and recall
that tainted tribe we were,
so fierce in Troy,
stirred by furies of time
and though hundreds the
years have passed since then,

that siege still haunts
my brain and proves my ken.
The victims strewn as wreckage
vowed return though
left on the bleakest shore,
somehow making a song

for every ear. These words
of the fallen fathers I hear,
a poem to recall and
recite, these words
you must have lost
to gain your modern sight:

See me Achilles,
great warrior found;
recall you shrank
from those battles
as Hector slew
our warring human souls

to make us see the gods'
cruelest wartime tolls.
So many brothers,
all those sisters died;
from the strength of gods
no act or voice replied.

Greek armies though
are armies of life
said Jove while still
no forces helped
us from above
when bodies were thrown

on piles in turn
until he reached
our ships, our dreams
to burn. We stood there,
left as Asia's refugees;
we wandered till Ajax

appeased our foes,
though his way was slow,
too slow for honor,
and Hector's passion ran
too far there free,
assured he'd die as

had his family;
and this has always
been our way in life,
too great our greed,
too deep our strife.
Some battles rage

without and some within
so Hector killed
Achilles' closest friend
to light a fire,
his mortal foe to send.
See them—the Trojans—

greeting the rage
of Achilles as he
entered that killing
cage, that place
we came to know
and to dread.

Revenge drove him
to slaughter men
and send them as
ghosts to a solemn
den for fallen bodies
and wounded souls.

It left Achilles and
Hector on that plain
to fight alone,
to chase down our
blood's last stain;
so there upon that

dismal scene were made
the conditions of
our time, the debt we
paid. Our hope shall
be ever fleeing,
bounding forth until

death—our fatal moment—
makes its sound.
And there I heard
the screams of history,
as if then Hector's
death mine own could see.

I saw his limp body,
freshly killed, dragged
around us all as his
slayer cruelly willed,
then heard his broken
father beg its return,

and saw the way
the furies spurned
his life. All the gods
had fought this brutal
war with us, as life itself
our bodies with hatred tore;

for while today
you'll not remember me,
we both once fought
to set our spirits free.
You've asked yourself
how this now lights

your modern way:
thoughts still obey
these emotions; forget
lost Troy, care nothing
of our human throng,
dismiss its lessons

now dressed in song;
yet you were there
in wars of blood
and steel, and now
as then no hero will
those fields reveal

but force itself,
who'll cut all
flesh and time
to use our fate,
our hopes to climb,
and crush all hopes

that sadness can
endure—force, the
beast who make
its timeless way
and, by our actions,
a lasting life assure.

AESCHYLUS IN CHORUS

Chorus:

We now will sing
    for our own
        and show the darkness
            of the heart,

show the Divine,
    how He drew Helen here,
    how we were blind
        to follow her

as love would lure
    and make us rush;
        we, drawn by luxury,
            by grace,

to death of ships,
    of men and dreams.
        What vengeance pulled us
        all this way

when proudly we
    sang bridal songs
        and arm in arm
            we crashed the seas,

as life by life
  we gladly died?
    Past Troy we happily
      ventured then,

we kinsmen and we brothers strong,
  past seas and cities
    we tread—a vast run,
      a voyage to our deaths.

Beyond the farthest
  span of earth
    we walked to dreams
      of places calm

and heard the winds
  of crying souls.
    The beasts of rage
      devoured us

and spared so few
  that dying sense.
    It was the fatal lure
      of Helen's eyes,

the smile masking
  bad intent,
    like Iphigeneia's
      so deep,

that child of flames
    with skin so soft
        who mixed and lured
            our hate with love;

and Agamemnon
    was subtly flawed,
        as gilded houses
            will hide dust,

as coins and smiles
    disarm men,
        and singing forecasts
            the human fate.

A death cry now
    is reminding us
        of a murder unlike
            the others we've known

and the past instructs
    a future there,
        the way it must
            and always has.

I stand here stunned
    by Clytemnestra,
        her arrogance,
            her brutal heart;

and we who killed
for false honor,
I sing now loudly
for our guilt

as this death we have
brought home, the killers
after ten years of blood;
yet I recall our ships once new,

our brittle hopes
unbroken once,
that dreamt return
with native pride,

and not infectious
failure's way;
for all in life
warns of that end,

that we, as men,
have lived to die.

THE INVITATION OF SOPHOCLES

Gather spirits
   of human souls
      and tell me your
         sacred inner goals,

quell my despair,
   my gloomy ways,
      to share that grail
         on which you gaze,

or fill my ear
   with a golden dust
      so that past this life
         my mind may trust.

Say not this day
   to my life confines,
      that in my chest
         mere want repines,

that vengeance as
   mere hunger lives,
      that hate no
         lasting evil gives;

and born of bodies
   though not ending so,
      tell me where
         our spirits go,

by what path,
　　what timeless clue;
　　　　for once I thought
　　　　　　I knew this true—

that somehow this
　　had music shown
　　　　and melody
　　　　　　had heaven known,

not lower realms
　　of food and wine;
　　　　yet when I traced
　　　　　　her upward line,

I did not find
　　your spirit home,
　　　　but places restless
　　　　　　hopes would roam.

Music became
　　atonal then
　　　　as there I found
　　　　　　its darkened den

thus freed of man's
　　assertive sense,
　　　　unleashed from earthly
　　　　　　joys so dense

and with no ancient
　　rites to seek
　　　　or human senses
　　　　　　strong and meek.

I knew I'd never
    find you there,
        high in music's
            secret lair,

so now I seek
    your higher grail
        where all things born
            of earth will fail.

EURIPIDES AS THE GODDESSES QUARREL

Goddess Aphrodite:

Give me always
    the saw of Sophocles:
        that while he showed us
            as we ought to be,

it was my greater son,
    Euripides,
        who always showed us as
            we truly are.

From this emerged
    his form of Hippolytus
        who is happy only
            in a life of nothings;

and from this came the
    lust of Phaedra,
        a stepmother who her
            own son pursued,

who caused treacheries,
    son to father.
        I placed there in his hands
            some human truths

but let him mold them
    as he pleased; so Phaedra
        he made famous
            in her death,

yet found her suffering
    from an inner weight.
        He listened to me
            when I warned him so—

that the doors of death
    would open to his hero,
        and he heard me, that the father
            would hunt his son

and that this son
    would accuse his mother's lust,
        then he bowed to me when shown
            that passion rules this animal.

Goddess Artemis:

Listen not to her!
    I am the child of Leto,
        condemning those figures
           of clay you're asked to praise.

The least poor Thesus,
    sinning through misfortune,
        yet more his son whose
           noble soul proved his ruin;

still much in their suffering
    there was for me to love;
        so into their mouths I spoke
           some timeless prayers,—

to the father, that he would
    embrace his dead son,
        unknowing was his
           murder of the boy;

to the son, that he would
    not then harbor hatred,
        for by fate he died and
            not by his father's hand.

Believe these final words
    spoken to his father:
        This is the end
            of what I have to bear,

I am gone,
    cover my face up quickly.
        And mind the view
            of Hippolytus,

not the sexual, lurid ways
    of Aphrodite.
        Recall that my hero
            spurned her strong advances

and thus compelled
    her suicide for shame;
        place in your mind that boy,
            so pure that day

but do not,
    as my rival would insist,
        be haunted by her
            vessel's ghostly lust.

ARISTOPHANES AFLOAT IN AIR

This morning
    was truer
        than others have been
            for a cloud

and its maidens
    who arose
        in their array,
            those infinite forms,

yet no one,
    not even the birds,
        saw them when they emerged
            as living, earthly restatements

of an ancient promise—
    so no soul could know
        how they floated so freely
            up over mountain bluffs and trees below,

or how they drifted with the vapors
    that cooled the cauldrons
        of an eastern wind;
            but truly they were sailing

and surely they were there,
    gliding so high, past roads reddened and curved
        till they descended slowly
            into a forest,

with firs and with aspen,
    all life teeming;
        then fulfilled, ascended once more
            to the air,

only to land again,
    this time on a beach with its song
        and listen to the percussions
            of the sea and its waves;

yet when this happened, this thing true,
    they thought of life's leisure and died with a peace,
        because the rain had shown them the reason
            that they had lived.

PART TWO

and the Romans say it is exposed at the time of death . . .

LUCRETIUS, TO QUELL OUR
FEARS OF DEATH

Ask me not
   of death—
      I know you have fears—
         read Epicurus,

take his advice
   and assume
      with him our poor
         trapped souls will die

as will our bodies
   by time's assault,
      then remove all fault
         from this fact of ours.

Now witness those tides
   of horror that rise
      in you, for yourself
         and all those others you'd love true.

Ask what drives this terror
   that you now feel,
      and finally see
         the nature of dreading—

that what you fear
   is not death, for death is nothing,
      nor even a time when you'll not be,
         for you don't lament

those days before you lived,
   those millions
      of barren lifeless years
         before you.

Now lay those infinites down,
   deep within your fearing mind,
      and let the lifeless before
         comfort its lifeless son.

VIRGIL AND THE CUTTING OF A HAIR

Each time that Dido lifted her fallen head,
    all three times, she fell back upon her bed;
she tried to open those eyes then closed to day,
    but as she saw the light in pattering play,
she closed them quickly as one too sick to see,
    resigning herself to fate's unfelt decree,
until to her side flew Juno's grieving soul
    to end that pain of death in living toll,

and sent her Iris to thwart the long despair,
    her struggling body far beyond repair,
with hopes that since she'd die not by a crime
    or heaven's judgment but by the fate of time,
this final punishing blow she would be spared
    to free her soul, a better home prepared,
and Juno prayed so deep for this from love,
    the rage who'd brought despair, the rage above;

so in that moment the goddess toward her moved,
    to by that dying lover's head have proved
compassion clear as her last action true.
    She softly said unto those gods she knew,
Take this daughter of mine, offer to thee,
    into thy home of the dead, thy place of the free,
and she cut the fatal hair that held the earth
    to Dido's soul, as did the human birth
of one whose need was the final escape from strife
    and the lasting release of a beauty ensnared by life.

HORACE, FATE AND THE SEWING OF TIME

There are times
	by fortune sewn and made
which—once revealed—
	it seems that destiny's laid,

those ways so hidden
	there and so unknown.
Recall though seeker,
	when this stitch is shown,

when I, blind fate,
	will smite thy saddened dreams,
that this is not
	what all at first it seems;

and permit not insolence
	to show its inward swell
when to it falls
	the crest of nature's spell;

recall the remote
	woodlands where once thou roamed,
the places of pine
	and circling streams that foamed;

recall those times
	when thou felt a subtle peace,
and still, even
	those homes won't hold life's lease,

for thou must die,
        this much was always true,
as will depart
        the things thou gathered too,

and ask what treasures
        could form from joys and wealth,
or boasts or acts
        or even body's health

when on that final
        night thou shall then be
alone there in
        thy grave as poor as me.

OVID'S DESCENDING TALE

Along through ages a tale descends
and floating softly to me intends,
to settle sentient in my way
and ever in your mind now stay.
By it, if believed as something true,
the saints would then God's errands do,
and often leave their darkened cells
to walk about the village dells;
so once in Kent did two men stroll
to try the people as a whole
and dressed as hermits by dimmest light,
were sacred brothers that wint'ry night.

Thus coldly, house to house, they wander'd,
disguis'd in habits they quietly saunter'd,
each door a woeful image made,
and hoping pity they'd then be paid;
yet the beggars were turned that evening back
as neighbors missed their saintly track,
not one devout invit'd them in
or cared to give them warmth within
till to a cottage those beggars came,
the home of a yeoman much the same
who then was Philemon the Honest call'd,
He's good though old, one boy recall'd.

He asked those saints that coldest eve,
to rest a while and not to leave,
then lit a fire there to cook,
and from his chimney happ'ly took
a piece of bacon large and fat,
whose slices wide then popped and spat,
and filled their jugs up to the top,
insisting that they drink each drop.
By his kindness they were amaz'd
and soon into his eyes they gaz'd,
for the ways his humble heart had mov'd,
the depth that night his soul had prov'd;

and as the evening made its close,
they broke their masquerade to foes.
Sir, we're Saints, the hermits said,
and made him feel at once misled,
until to him they would relate
his destiny, his flip of fate,
that he would not be harm'd at all,
though others who'd not heard their call
a spiteful end would savage seize,
for they, their homes and families
were water bound and all soon drown'd,
while his abode would then be crown'd
a rising citadel and a church,
to nobly sit by heaven's perch.

PART THREE

but the Italians acquaint it with life,
with music and art and love . . .

DANTE'S RETURN

I've now returned as my poems once foretold,
to courtyards here where peasants mutter my name
and where museums of Florence praise my time.
I recall those days I walked with life and sight
and see how great is the grief awaiting me here;
recall those brighter days of primal joy
that came before colossal miseries;
and now, upon this stone, among these birds,
weep as memory cruelly retells my tale,
remaking first the look of my stillborn pen,
then making it murderous when placed within my hand
and married to the parchment on my desk.
What scars, memory, were made from this scene
and who here knows those voices I heard then?

Who, I now ask these many ages hence,
has read my deathbed words of life's great curse?
That *the rights of the Monarchy and the Heavens,*
the stream of the Fire and of the Immortal Pit
I saw in my visions and sang then to the Fates,
but since my soul was absent from me there,
I was happier somehow in death, having gone
to my mother above amid the eternal stars.
So on that day my living self was through
and exiled from those bare ancestral shores
of Florence, the lesser mother I had known.
My outward life became a failure then,
while inwardly a way was made by sadness.
I wrote to relinquish all those things of thee,
my most beloved, so the arrows I then sent
would be from bows of exile first of all,

and my bread would taste then not of mortal tears
but heavenly powers and of my mortal fears.
I ask the beggars within this crowded plaza,
What became of Dante Alighieri?
He was a writer, mad from olden times,
says one quite drunk and sitting on the street.
He saw my future, a tour or way to Hell,
a tortured path down to an ordered world
so tainted by sin, and showed me there, you ghost,
how both our spirits have always been corrupted.
And then the beggar slurring these strange words
drinks again and coughs and talks with birds.

All this is shown by cruel memory,
how I walked through afterlife, there with a guide,
fond Beatrice who died back in my youth
but then became eternal, a holy spirit
to watch me and to guide me through those realms,
Inferno, Purgatory, Paradise,
those chambers deep through which I with her passed;
and on this journey saw the reasoning men
betraying reason and thus betraying Him,
saw living there those sinners of all kinds,
down deep to the base of a vast and fiery Hell,
that place where they'd endure unspeakable fates,
and where I saw Ulysses, so resourceful,
there in his filthy home so unremorseful.

Back in the plaza I meet a peasant woman
acknowledging me as man and not as ghost.
She tells me of actors who live in *Dante's Hell*
appearing disguised as leopard, lion and wolf,
those earthly sins of appetite, spirit and reason,
and how they had denied her just salvation.
She mumbles to me in lowly words and ways,
deriding those agents of Hell *who spake so badly,*
misusen' all ther words and like me brother

just grumblin' and moanin' and cursin' at me so
when understood, and the rest of it's just sounds,
ther spits and screechins, like some vicious hounds.

Speak and hear, I tell her as she stares
and then describe to her the look of Hell,
the ways it showed me and its gruesome state.
She looks upon her poor and sunken home,
peers around, looks back and says to me:
You savage ghost, you should by God be damned,
you know you've just described this hatin' earth,
this city, this fam'ly, this strugglin' life of mine!
and by her piercing curse I finally sense
that she sees as Hell, this earth in every tense.
Amid all this, this hating condemning scene,
I tell them all, the peasants, of escapes for all
through paths of love and through our human bonds,
fraternal strength and hopeful light of faith;
but now they swell as one and they attack me
and beat me to the ground, with kicks and grunts
and spit themselves until I feel the fading
of an empty, saddened life once made for Him,
and can feel by fate there silenced for all of time
a voice for God who spoke in human rhyme.

ADDRESS OF THE SEQUESTERED
BOCCACCIO

To you, ladies, my address should be clear
and please, dear Petrarch, forgive my speech,
for you'll not my Decameron now hear,
but a remembrance it did beseech,
how ten long days could once appear
as living tales my mind would reach.

Before I could write the Filocopo,
the Filostrato or love's kin,
I fell in love myself to know
remorse, desertion's child, love's twin,
for Troilus adored Cressida so
but it was my misery his love would win.

I sadly sang his human despair
as matched laments my life has known,
sought what his tears and sighs repair,
past agonies, past all that they have sown;
and wrote of Cressida's charms so fair
to sing of my lover's beauty alone.

Decameron our inner lives thus bore
from minds retreating plagues so dense,
those hints our lives there hid by lore;
in days we spent in present tense;
I watched as all the earth could implore
found its way into our sense.

We sang not of the Divine, its glow,
nor primal strings of perfect men,
but rather of those fruits we knew
were borne our tree in seasons ten,
plain moments that would life bestow,
that taste, that grace beyond my pen.

MICHELANGELO LOOKING UPWARD IN THE SISTINE CHAPEL

My future distant friend, you must now see me,
the starving cat who's up from stagnant streams,
and see this lonely denizen of dreams
who wanders aimless, fated among the free.

Come see my nape, how inward it would be
when with my bones and spine, my supple limbs,
it forms an instrument for Godly hymns
surpassing every word and earthly plea.

Witness also my muscles that gather and gleam
in skin that cups my frame, suspending me so,
a human lyre that's played both sonorous and true.

This music-maker, Sir, would ever seem
hung below a ceiling to notes bestow;
and give the vault of God rhymes ever new
        when images by me He threw,
and those inhuman tones He did here sound,
all prophets of His coming shouting round.
        See then Sir, what I have found
and hear in paint my songs for the birth of man
as one lone servant's voice did strain to span.

PART FOUR

and the Spaniards and Latin Americans believe
firmly that it lies between the inner self and outer world . . .

CERVANTES' APOLOGY FOR FRIENDS

As they were alien heroes in clashing worlds these two,
their journeys to glorious realms would when as one ensue;
first for me the errant knight to us revealed
a wide blue ocean we call the self so oft' concealed,
and seemed larger, stronger, more forceful all those days
than all the others, for by Action he made his vital forays
and used his Will so all the rest to him would bend.
Look next to my realist who rides beside the knight to their end,
as by our selves the outer realms we know will be led;
and while into our minds both these turbid streams are fed,
one from within and the other from an unknown outer realm,
the inner it seems would always that other overwhelm.
Take Don, who suffered from this outer world divorce,
but while insane, had a spirit from an inner source,
and who oft' heard Sancho but was not by him ever bound
for his purpose within, his worth, even his sight or sound.
Still, what the thought that could without its body live,
and how hard the world where forms don't to our dreams life give?
So in this subtle way they wander upon this earth
to give each other a purpose and each life its worth.

In these waters nature has placed our human feet;
we have the knight's ideals, there aloft in defeat;
we are strident beings despite our odds of life,
for we will always hope that things to our lives reserve
and daily struggle to our sacred things preserve.
Laugh first, then squarely look at my puppet surely broken
as you would see yourself were soulful truths there spoken.
See that outer world you have bravely battled
if even by deceits of it were you then rattled.
And there, in Sancho Panza find yourself as well,
a Seer riding reason not some dreamer's swell.
Recall that sharp remark often made of my book,
that it is but a group of stories lacking structure,
merely one illusion's hoax and then some other.
To this defect I surely now to you admit,
yet you must compare the life to which you now submit,
those fragments of a time lived not as piecemeal stories,
but a flowing life, made both of windmills and of glories.
And so, this riddle of life to you and I'll be done:
if our two worlds must merge, are my men there two or one?

NERUDA'S YOUTHFUL JOURNEY

I remember being alive through secret words,
a young bohemian poet in Santiago
who ranged from silence to rain like a penance.
I collected goods from the markets of avarice,
those tainted remnants of humanity transfixing the very air,
and used images from my bog-dweller days,
the wild water blossoms, the green forest corridors.
All these stark quintessences of life devoured me
and set my mind ablaze, parting it from fate's course
as if ravished serenities had the power to alter
the harrowed symmetries of time's cadence.
Each day my body fell a certain way while
my spirit was deflected down pits and passageways
meant for those who'd become estranged from themselves.
In these days, I saw not only a ghostly being arise
but witnessed births of being in the poems,
saw them arise, wrenching out of my human grip
to stand full before me, no longer silences
or even children of my images but harbingers
announcing some other boundless, coming world.

These were the naked forces that separated
me from myself and wasted my regenerations
as I sped through the bones of the poets before me,
learning to loathe the beautiful as I cherished
the passing travails of my most inward moments.
There were in those days real savageries about me
but even these my poems asked me to bury
as there were true human impulses they dealt with,
compelling me to tear even them away from myself.
What I was left with from all this I barely recall.
I know I encountered death and its appendages
as I grazed the sides of those channels I sped down.
I know I opened vast, immeasurable doorways
as I looked back to the alien limits of my human life.

MARQUEZ WANDERING A MUSEUM

On exile from Colombia, a place no longer free,
    I wandered lifeless into some museum hall
where Dali's *Apparition* somehow spied me,
    and heard from it the plea from Time to us all:
that in ancient days the gods a service did do
    to check the hands that painted earth-born forms;
but now they bind the soaring art of we few
    who seek to show the mind, its force and storms;
these gods were thus offended on that day
    when Dali in paint showed a mind the eyes can't see.
Some laughed aloud while his hands began to play,
    for he painted what a mental world had begged to be:
a dog, its collar, objects made so plain,
    but described by the eye of mind as lawless then,
and seemed to form a mountain and bridge for some train
    by a bay, a human face—yet who knows when?
This artist flouts all nature, chuckled one god.
    Yet look, he nears us! said another with a nod.

I saw Macondo when those gods walked in;
    and there in paint saw fictions, the lands of my clan
where Arcadio could by my novel Ursula win,
    where two sons born to them enlarged the plan,
for the boys had sons and the father's name each bore,
    so there was from each Arcadio yet another,
from one Aureliano eighteen more,
    and each was proud to have the name of his brother.
But as these gods of Dali surveyed that scene
    they condemned my flock and cursed its maddened days,
then asked me if those two had cousins been
    and laughed about their nightly wrestling ways,
retold how Ursula at first beat Arcadio back
    until he took her in her bed one night,
despite her fears and worries that from this attack
    iguanas might be born to seal their plight.
Those gods then asked me why she'd daily shrunk
    until the children mistook her for a doll
and how she died . . . as if reality were drunk,
    not only for this creature but for all.
It's absurd! yelled one great god who dared to stare.
    But it's man's first world! said another to be fair.

PART FIVE

yet listen to the early English who say it has a meter matching
nature's . . .

CHAUCER'S REFLECTIONS
ON HIS PILGRIMAGE

For I'd hadde been y-this, ne'er seyde thee Host,
Yet Canterbury pilgrimage layd bare,
A prymerd be beten my mind the most.
By trewe moments this felawe gan did preye,
Whan on yong and tender my early deye
I saw these tales of myrthe in human place,
Saw Knight and Millere, coude Pardoner's face.
    These travels me sith changed, answerde me thus:
Some thyngs unto ye shal by lyf I shew,
Some miracles al men in time wol knowe
And by my legends this smal trouthe is told,
Lyves beste rym I wol mak in houres bold,
As Cressida did sey, I wol be trewe,
Or Pardoner did vow to not deceive you.
    This song maked in reverence of wan age
Asks of ye reder fond, beyond my stare:
By what countenance, in whose language,
Do you by me constrewe and lyf declare?
As I, so you, lyves trials do repare,
And as yer lost Host did so laff and boast,
So wol thee of this human comedie toast.

WYATT BURNING HIMSELF

If this day your woeful heart shall tire,
though mine remains here bound to thee,

if that honest will still aches in me
or my visage incites your burn of ire,
if unchained becomes your beast desire
or my voice, once in tune and free,

must discordant in your ear now be;
or if you forsake what we attire

and to another than myself hold dear,
dismissing all my sighs repeatedly
for anger that is fed incessantly;
and if this fire so cold though near

is what by love I'd now burn in strife,
I'll seek instead the warmth of life.

SIDNEY ON WRITING

Drawn by stars and graceless speech I'd fain here show,
That my Stella might someday see the love that I possess
And all virtues of pleasure on her in dreams I would bestow,
To then match her halting form, her subtle frame to bless;
Yet I wrote in pain, hoped pain would cause her this to know:
That all showers of light, all forms that nature'd ever dress,
Have betrayed my truant pen from which no beauties flow
And on lifeless sands I sought her essence to possess,
As if now, in less life her full life I'd somehow find as prey;
But past this nature the pen within my hand there froze
Until my fault the moon did show to me and say,
For it asked me how each day my mind by speech love throws.
 By invention, nature's child! I cried to the moon's soft light.
 You must look within, it said and freed my mind to write.

SPENSER AND THE CONQUERING OF BLISS

1

Hear my second book, the seventh canto,
whence passing forth I verily retold
Sir Guyon's moral legend so you'd know
how self-control and temperance unfold,
when wrought here by a visit then so cold
as had pertained that power, the Bower of Bliss,
by which he met his bare and natural mold;
and pity you'd find, spectacle resist a
delight which by his pleasure would insist.

2

All this my Palmer dreamt, more by his gate,
battles not of force but sensual sin
and images of genius, proudest human state,
the ancient voice, the sage of ours within
and of its counsel, our inner sense to win:
that each within us has a phantom true,
a guide of the self, transparent inner kin
who by its wondrous ways shall ever do
those acts that conquer bliss, its comely rew.

3

Hear those heavens and hear their ways so jovial
as you look upon their still and steadfast state,
enjoy those spacious plains where his feet would fall.
Ready yourself for battle, your simple fate,
prepare your mind to search and moderate;
see your foe, her form, where beauty would dwell,
her gifts, the cup of gold to operate,
the fruit by which she will impeach so well,
her ecstasy, a guise to seal your hell.

MARLOWE RESPONDING TO
THE VOICE IN RALEGH'S REPLY

Let me respond, my nymph of love,
   so you may now our pleasures prove
      as promised in wood, in field and hill,
         and live with me, our love to fill.

I asked for you upon the rocks,
   gazed to shepherds there with flocks;
      and you replied, *by time they're old*,
         recast my rocks a place so cold.

My dream was then your bed of roses,
   laced therein with leaves and posies;
      victims for you that time has gotten,
         seen as things that are soon rotten.

My *belt of straw and ivy buds*,
   and *coral clasps with amber studs*,
      you'd find in them no slightest thrill
         nor live with me, our love to fill.

Surely as is said of summer fields,
   a reckoning way the winter yields;
      and flowers fade, you know this true,
         through time will all our gifts pass through.

Yet should you not now be my love
   and delight these things that we would move,
      you'd miss this joy for time will kill,
         so live with me, our love to fill.

SHAKESPEARE'S INVITATION
FROM THE WAVE

Before I sang of waves to a pebbled shore
As spirits in time or minutes marching ahead,
I followed Marlowe on stage, his poet's rapport,
The way he'd force to life those things once dead;
And while I feel what waters daily teach
With unregretful ways and simple sounds,
I once heard only dry and human speech,
Until when acting felt life's tides in rounds.
My player life is more the way of waves,
The love that crests to know and then is lost,
Than of a song or other earth-bound slaves
Who by their tongues and minds are timely tossed.
So still I must express myself this way!
I rise, invite and with a flow decay!

DONNE TO THE APPROACHING VISITORS

Whenever to my grave you approach to mourn,
        do not question
my strange way, that sense so lost and forlorn;
for now another life my body's won;
        see this, great matter's toll,
what he has slain, my beauty and my art,
        each vestige of my soul
when this body these bones he'd not depart.

Do not despair my decayed and slender thread,
        so broken to dust,
that spawned love and joy, pain and senses dead;
a thin mind's hair, once grown by only trust,
        the faith that I'd be whole,
one being, not the millions of these lines
        this rotted brain time stole,
the vestiges returned as my tomb a soul confines.

Toss all I hoped or knew within that coffin,
        for I am then
as that dark case, worth what is within;
cast there those forms once born my mental ken
        and then I'll by you win
the goal of having every piece there dead
        laid by its mental twin,
of being complete, though of all life thus bled.

HERRICK AS TIME FLIES

I'd not be one who looks on naive
        while time with you is flying;
the flowers now you closely cleave,
        tomorrow they'll be dying.

If sooner displays the strong sun's light,
        then sooner it is setting;
the clearer a thing is there in sight,
        the closer its end is getting.

That age is best which we had first,
        and warmer's blood when younger;
for by our time we're each day cursed
        when less becomes our hunger.

So virgins, take this day made new
        and to you it will comply,
for shown by our sun, our time's late hue,
        your dim, aged self will die.

HERBERT APPROACHING BATTLE

Lo! there's a battle ahead my Lord,
    yet I am broken,
    and still not woken,
once a poor creature, now wonder stored,
    soon to travel in space and light
    from earth to heaven's grace so bright.

Betwixt my world and yours my Lord,
    furies do rage,
    my soul to cage;
as life in my body once you poured,
    now fears this void will soon replace,
    as stern grave fighters my soul will face.

Oh Lord, while once I'd inner guides,
    they've quit their place
    by heaven's pace;
all human thoughts and jealous prides
    will now attack my broken frame
    in battles formed of same on same.

So face these cursed fighters Lord,
    kill them and me
    so I may see
that place to which my guides have soared;
    expose your plan, my fate sublime,
    my soul devour for all in time.

Then if this is your will my Lord,
my soul here broken,
your lowly token,
see it in heaven gently moored
as it invites an inner light,
its battle blessed by loving sight.

VAUGHAN IN MISTS OF PAST

So strange the days in mists of past,
when time would ever then so last;
part object, part essence was that place,
the life before this second race.
Those days my soul a heaven sense
did bless, but lacked this earthly tense
and only loved that purest being
who dwelt within, ought eyes for seeing;
my body then had not yet breathed,
nor lungs begun their end or seized.
As young again I would reflect
and back to life my thoughts inspect,
a celestial face my mind would show
a presence warm, His after-glow.
Out then from every timely way
I heard eternity to say:
depart my splinter to return,
become a thing, a hint to learn.
Before my words brought hate to me
or actions set my sins out free,
I was at peace, not time's sad tool
nor fated so as sin's fine fool,
one whose powers could then be felt
that mystic seers once had spelt;
early, ageless, that breath of life,
not this pleading, dogged strife;
and what I'd give to walk once more,
looking back on life's first door;
but now my soul by time is changed,
stumbling where once it freely ranged.
Still, I sensed through a final glance
that I'd known all this in some primal trance.

MILTON WITH REMNANTS OF HIS GOD

My God was scattered about me in sanctities and glories;
   He was spoken in utterances every day received
which my mind had formed so free, ordained and known,
   and made this prayer, this shadow of my fate:
that I would one day be writing upon His altar
   with that inner hallowed fire, that lasting passion

and steady observation as befits
   a Homer, Sophocles, Pindar or perhaps
as Virgil once had sung with solemn music;
   and to this impulse then fell ancient images
in stanzas blank with epic form and power.
   This work imagined me to redraw Eden

as it must have been beside the early wars
   of giants, the fighting gods, with me and all,
from heroes of Homer and ways of Aeschylus
   to Tasso, to Arthur and to the Song of Roland,
and all these passed as leaves fell in our forest
   when frost first came upon the human autumn.

Sweet was Eve's first speech, her rising sense,
   as if God had spoken to her in ways we'd know,
and cursed was Satan, our inner apostate angel,
   though sublime as desire he surely would always be.
I saw him change from a radiance to an evil,
   dwelling there as he must in penal fires,

chained as he is to shores of a burning lake.
   Yet, from these images of mine the problems arose,
for Hell is both that place of all our torment

and Satan's greatest battle ground for our souls,
so within this diversity of things his nightmare lives.
   Again was I shown my God, his radiant light

and I could hear Him truly as he spoke to me,
   as He blamed Adam and Eve for our every fall,
as then He persecuted them to their awful fate
   before a second coming there by His grace.
All this to know that God used their sin for us,
   that we might someday dwell in a fonder Eden.

So I wrote their end to new beginnings make
and wandered their Eden in my lonely way.

DRYDEN TO THE LOVERS

No lover need decide
    that he is glad though poor,
    that lesser things are more;
and smooth through life she'll slide,
    though not a gem she'll store.
For in her mind resides
as in his gaze confides
those joys from high above,
the pleasures of their love.

My poems this should prove
    if made from my own days
    as lovers they would praise;
and what I might thus move
    is past my shortened gaze.
These words fly high and fall
to hearts that so would call
those joys from high above,
the pleasures of their love.

POPE'S WILL OF GOD

Far as man's keen mind has ranged and wandered,
over those vast and foreign lands it's pondered,
of complexities, quandaries and their kind,
none conform to instinct or truth unwind
as the study of man, the maker of our senses,
that vital search not swayed by faith's defenses;
for while reason unwraps the mind and tempts the soul,
the search for God we cannot hope control.
    Trust dear truth though we will, pray when we can,
    God's world we must divide from that of man.

PART SIX

and the modern English and Irish who claim its
language is not of words . . .

WORDSWORTH WATCHING
PROTEUS EMERGE

See Proteus now emerging from the sea
and confess to him all your alien ways:
that you have not seen nature's mighty forays
into that universal place so free!
Hear Triton, his horn with its great and ageless decree.
When, ask him, did you give your own heart away?
How, you should ask, could you have forsaken this day?

Out of tune with him, ask to see
how you have wasted your deepest human powers;
ask to hear the sea, the whispers of wind,
know much there is in nature to be ours.
Learn earth's language, human words rescind,
place within your mind images past hours
and be not by nature one more deathly pinned.

COLERIDGE REFORMING HIS DREAM

. . . But then, this Xanadu of Kubla Khan,
whose broad and stately pleasure-dome arose,
was re-formed as new again and its form re-drawn
as numbly back I fell to break upon
     a bleak and lifeless repose.
And in that state I passed those prescient hills
so ancient and out beyond my human thrills
where blossomed many a fruit and flower tree,
and where I gazed from the grasp of time set free.
That place re-made replaced all things for me
in worlds thus wrought by its scene of greenery.
     An arching curve this made one aching day,
the way a life is limitless and long when exposed,
so each moment a savage presence would mindless pray
till I heard a wail for a demon-lover that way,
     as lifeless I reposed.
In this place of pain and disease, the place of life's bid,
where the sense beneath my reaper's blade had hid,
and from these mighty mountains, those fragments of war,
and by that stream, I heard a faint refrain,
an ancestral voice beneath a cavernous floor,
one who sang to me with deep disdain:
     Then all the charm
is broken—all that phantom-world so fair
vanishes, and a thousand circlets spread,
and each mis-shapes the other. Stay awhile,
poor youth! who scarcely dar'st lift up thine eyes—
the stream will soon renew its smoothness, soon
the visions will return! And lo, he stays,
and soon the fragments dim of lovely forms
come trembling back, unite, and now once more
the pool becomes a mirror.

BYRON DANCING

1
She came last evening but a trace,
    as time glanced smooth upon her skin,
a nimble nymph of Grecian grace;
    all destiny it seemed her eyes could win.
Her form thus brought me to that place,
    cold to call, of heaven's kin.

2
A curse I'd find and fact I'd see:
    that my cousin hid beneath her mask
and all our ball was pagan plea
    from dateless dream to timeless task.
So, soft and slow she danced by free
    as there I stood, her ne'er to ask.

3
But sliding down her slender form,
    so faint, so fresh, as yet unbroken,
her essence drew and would adorn
    hints of heaven, my distant omen,
and put the drive to love forlorn,
    back within my soul again.

KEATS AND THE SONGS OF THE
SUN-DRENCHED HILLS

Many are the songs of the sun-drenched hills
    never heard by minds blanketed in sleep
and the teller who this eludes, all kills
    by strokes of time cutting so deep;
rhyme-less songs sung on an urn,
    the legends silent words would show,
eternal struggles red clay reforms:
    eros, bliss . . . taint time's glow
while distant gods eachother spurn
    and sing o'er hills past human storms.

A youth upon this fired place,
    beneath a tree, eternal and still,
had his love captured in space.
    His sensual and yet undying will
hung untouched though near the hand of his lover,
    and beside him flutists feigned a note,
but they are as we to some far off God:
    creatures in spirit, in time afloat—
they on an urn, we on this sod,
to show what's past the heart's endeavor.

SHELLEY'S LAST QUESTIONS

1

And if winter comes but no spring follows...
What then? What trumpet sounds by this wind?
What autumnal being moves as it blows?

It's a fleeing evil, a thing that's sinned,
far worse than pestilence may bring. O thou,
great taker, riding on a time soon dead!

Wild spirit, why move us to earth, great plow?
And why, destroyer, do you mock these hours,
not sister or brother but orphan now?

Why whisper o'er the dreamless coffers?
By what power, this force of death, by whom?
What drives me past all stillness offers?

Deadening spirit who art life's tomb,
destroyer who'd not preserve me, oh, hear!

2

Thou by whose nature and changing way
the centuries bring sleet and darkened clouds,
thou wrought from a chaos as night from day.

What may we ask the approaching shrouds?
What can be said to the dying leaf?
That spring is close for sprouting crowds?

We cannot say this to one in grief
as it matters not if spring finds winter
when blowing through me is absence, life's thief.

And if thy cold I'd now feel enter,
or if I'm wrapped in thine own remorse
or sense thy nameless, inhuman center,

I'll seek to find thy inner source,
for from death, as from life, all things flow!

3
Thou who breaks on the unseen sea,
the mover of grasses by the hidden way,
run beside last thoughts called free.

Tame-less impulse, virgin of day,
carry the white caps, the flying seeds
to fall where thou will ever lay.

Be my fate, my earthly needs!
Scatter my thoughts on barren ground
and sever my hope by deadly creeds.

Clarion call, make me thy sound,
commit me though restless ever to rest,
by thy withered leaves let me be found.

And wind of action, ending round
make me a winter as are made the rest.

SCOTT AND THE QUICKENING SPIRIT

Thou who came and fled for wood,
      who left for mountain climes,
thou a thing not understood,
      vanished as better times;
escaped from us when needed sorest
      as days to an elder friend,
fleeing homeward to a deeper forest,
      a darkness to make an end.

Human hands that guide life's course
      are bound behind us here
and voices beg a deafened source
      of injustice far and near.
We look to thee, quickening spirit,
      to what remains of thee;
for by this we shall so inherit,
      this way that we must be.

Time will quicken to our brave touch
      as all joy passes us;
as all of life is fleeting as such,
      yet the river's foam entrusts
a subtle secret as it dissolves:
      that it wasn't made to last
but, yes, to burst as it resolves
      to the water that is its past.

TENNYSON'S UNDYING DOVE

Jesus, dove of undying love,
     thy hidden face in mine,
     that sense so supple and fine,
hear my regret to thee above:

I failed thee in my wandering way
     and absence would thy presence prove;
     thy orb to spin and move
as all I'd know by thy light would play,

for thou art a sacred glory within,
     tender thy way of the lamb,
     as sacred water's dam,
thou art that water we parry in,

and secret sharer of human grief
     so flawed and wracked by pain,
     tell us of that portal to gain
by which we'd find our lasting relief.

Is it in prayer or humbled word
     when words from the meager throat
     may ask but not devote
and thine absence proves such prayer absurd?

Or will thou leave us forsaken here,
     our wills piled dead by our cumber,
     starved linnets gross in number
whose folly presented to us is clear?

How, we ask, will we die for thee,
             trapped in our world untrue,
             reborn by heaven's hue,
and O Lord, in death will thou have us see?

Will we then see the awakening Divine,
             that dawn thou made for us,
             and bless new worlds to trust,
becoming thee as your clothes so fine?

We have but faith, we cannot know,
             this lesser world we see;
             yet sense your truth shall be
what in first sight thy new light will show.

Forgive our grief, forgive our longing,
             these ways confused and wan
             as we ply your ground upon
that valley that is our morrow dawning;

and forgive my weak and lonely cry,
             that shows unworthiness;
             and words that fail to bless
thy deeper longings for me to try.

I heard it from a beggar's lips,
             again in blessed psalms,
             that thou will give us alms
to bear alone our dark eclipse.

Alms of higher love are these,
             by darkness alms unchanged,
             those fates by thee arranged,
final states thy soul to please.

BROWNING LOOKING TO THE SEA

Perhaps you can see her out on the sea.
No, to the left, that sail she'd be;
she's there, that white craft sailing to us.
True, I once called her a vision to trust,
but now she's mere wood and cloth to hold
another, warming one not cold,
a hull to hold lovers returning to the shore,
as if back from ecstasy to now once more

sleep together in this place with others,
having left as two within those covers,
explorers to a realm deep whose surface
is all our bodies may know or press;
and perhaps as they near us you'll see her,
my lost lover, and see her grace confer
upon each and every scene a quietude
as nature shows, as the dawn would allude

to a greater being, a firmer realm,
so too my lost lover will overwhelm;
and as that bark to our wind will respond,
a figure to eyes revealed so fond,
you may rightly turn to me and ask,
Why let another in her love now bask?
The answer's better seen then heard:
it is by the maker of ships assured

as he would start with a frame of balance
then foresee the water and carve its dance
from bow to stern and hull to lee;
he'd tell you of her great love for me,
the way in the same design it grew
to anticipate another birth anew
with me, her sea, her eternal place.
Yet upon that voyage then apace

some shuddering of hull and stays and mast
broke upon my soul so fast;
a truth known sure, some flaw inhered
within my design so clear appeared.
In this way, my friend, I did detect
some error our love would infect.
It was on our first voyage that we saw
this fatal dissonance, this awful flaw.

What ever shall we do love? she prayed,
and I took in that ship to be remade.
It was in Cairo that this all occurred,
where winded love and stays were heard,
and we sadly saw her future changed,
what fate had always thus arranged.
Our regretful look was not an end;
for we planned to remake her and to send

homeward word of her passing at sea,
and of my return alone to be
without my lost lover upon this land
while she became another whose hand
warmly received the loving touch
of some other, yet unseen sea as such,
and to smoothly glide in nature's wet fields,
so without that strain to wind she yields.

Ask me not who's that helmsman strong
who holds my lover and sails along
that blissful afternoon sea she remade
to love him! Still, while once we forbade
looking or blaming, even recalling
the former sail or Egyptian calling,
still tell me brother when they pass us here,
sitting upon this bluff, just as they near.

Remind me to look to her as she stands
and see her eyes turn to me on these lands
of our forgotten love and fated ways,
and ask me, that other self who prays
of such things, *Is not that man we see
you sir once under a sail so free?*
Yes, that's my lover, to us she'll sail,
but this is my place, to love and to fail.

ROSSETTI'S PRAYER

Tell me mother is this our end,
    this shadow of death, this sea beyond?
    And is that place our eternity fond?
Why to us would infinity God send,
we who'd not life hope defend?
    And why do you mouth a fisher's plea
    when he'd in silence just bless the dead,
those bodies sunk past the human mend?

Show me mother how it shall be
    when we careen on rocks so hard;
    prepare us for this clash of our souls
    within that turbulent place so marred,
and let me mother, dread life's goals
then yearn to know this bottomless sea.

HOPKINS STANDING IN A FIELD

Greatly does God, our God, show nature's heart,
   in fields that flow from the winds of a summer's day,
      in endless waves that greet their home and main;

their way is to find an inner, an issued part,
   time's tide in heaven—its pattern, pace and play,
      in each thing, its birth and growing, showing grief and gain.

As nature is made and an essence emerges there,
   so too a life escapes, some bounding prey
      and, in its end, to early states will strain,

as when a wave regrets and a voice would dare—
   God will reign.

HARDY'S DREAM OF THE THRUSH

I dreamt to see a moral sky
    the day my loss became more real,
some Godly arc to then decry,
    an answering truth to inward feel;
but torrents of rain brought a pall,
    and dark clouds cursed a hidden sun,
when first I heard that haunting call
    from this, my time having fully run.

My hand an outline came to be
    as then I outward ghostly flew
and the present century passed by free,
    as timeless things I saw and knew.
It spoke to me through time and toll
    when back I looked the closing gate,
so shocked to see my image roll
    to the feet of birds my eyes await.

A thrush had I become that day
    and sang as I began to cry,
a darkened creature there to say
    not of how or when or even why,
but sing a full-hearted evensong
    of a sun that was always masked to man
and to fling my soul there among
    the lifeless time that past me ran.

A passerby who saw me caroling,
    who heard my song and plaintive plea,
asked me then what hope-filled thing
    could make me sing with glorious glee.
I answered in the approaching eve
    as would a thrush in trembling song,
filled with hope one world he'd leave
    and to another in the end belong.

OWEN AND THE MILITARY MARCH

What look, what strange mixture is this
that shows that we've detached from them?
That they to us could as cattle exist,
marching to death, its darkened den?
While once they loved and laughed with us,
they dwell with things forever lost,
a place with no voices or person's trust
where the chorus of rifle screams is crossed.

What line do they pass leaving us so?
One made by our minds, not hearts or eyes,
to fall for us and for us to rise.
The brush of a lover's skin lets me know
the press of flesh and loving ways
and a desperate sense of final days.

DE LA MARE RETURNING TO THE CASTLE

He returned to that fateful place, our traveler,
  lured by shrills of the night,
and by masks of that moonlit memory,
  as shadows assault the light;
and finally he felt those inner presences
  clinging to a castle so cold;
voices unheard then, unheard now, yet calling
  and by sadness, regrets fully told.
Are you there? he asked by the stone of the wall.
  Their response welled up and then
shook him silently, shuddering from hell.
  He felt the warring souls of men,
the lifeless beings who backward call
  and return to castles cold
to find unseen sights and unheard guests.
  Are you there? he asked so bold
but their answers were quiet, their presences bare.
  That house called human past
held their visages prefixed and possible
  in bodies not to last
and our traveler's horse slowly prepared
  to take others to this place,
those other self-same seeking strangers
  who'd sense this traveler's face,
almost hear that inaudible sadness;
  then wait upon that stair,
listen in silence to visitors come
  and hope they'd say, *Are you there?*
Unstirring, they'd feel the echoes of that call,
  and they would hear these strangers
mount their horses, hear shoes clap on stone

and be with silent dangers
that surge back, sound and sight receding;
then hear another say,
Tell them I came, and no one answered,
that I kept my word this day.

YEATS FEELING THE COOL WATER

First I'll feel the cool water, feel it on Lough Gill's shore,
and then I'll embark and paddle, paddle to Innisfree Isle
where a cabin waits, though waiting twelve by twenty four,
and there I'll stay for a long, long while.

As father said of Thoreau, my beans will a peace make grow
and that peace will speak to me through veils of a morning dew
as it once had done for one who asked what his woods could know
on that eve, the first of his days made new.

I'll then hearken back here, here to this bleak and urban day,
and recall I heard lake water whose sounds once called to me;
to know wherever I stand or by standing when to peace I pray,
this water laps in human key.

JOYCE TELLING OF PASSING FRIENDS

Stephen Dedalus:
Won't you come to Sandymount,
Madeline the Mare?
I have come to hear you shout
random thoughts we bear;
walk along eternity
Aristotle too;
crush, crack, crick modality
will gallop our minds straight through.

Join us now some father dear,
walk down to the beach;
tell me of my mother's fear,
me within her reach.
Wombed in sin's darkness she,
ghostly her ashen breath;
but it is He who has willed me
and cannot cause my death.

Tell me here at Sandymount,
Madeline the Mare,
if God is but a one to count
or the part of Christ less fair.
I'll invite good Arius
to ponder here this view;
I'll feel him with that cresting wave
and never shall need you!

The Bishop I will meet instead,
ask him now to show
that I am *idea* as he has said,
that no world of things we know;
that I am like a virgin clear,
so touch me with soft, sad eyes.
Softer hand, I'm lonely here,
touch me soon—arise!

Leopold Bloom:
I venture out to my home, the Dublin streets
and out here I feel so alone, seeking my place.
I wonder where Stephen is, now another image,
and on and on this present, and another present.
Not to worry, another replaces that one,
until a young man hands Mr. Bloom a pamphlet:
What? *Bloo* . . . you say? Me? Oh no.
Blood of the Lamb. Oh. Throw it away;
and his eyes show water's image to replace the words.
How can you own water? It's always in a stream.
My eyes say, *Post No Bills. Post No Bills.*
Some chap is here with a dose burning him . . . .
Mr. Bloom moves forward, raising his troubled eyes,
and a thought picks up that image and moves it aside.
(Think no more about that, Mr. Bloom.)
When I die, I wonder what will happen then . . .
but I'm alive, no need to wonder about that now.
(Give him another image, please.) Who's that?
O, Mr. Bloom, how are you today?
I'm well, and how do you do, Mrs. Breen?
O, about the funeral Mr. Bloom . . .
and I hear, *Your funeral is tomorrow*
while you are coming, coming through the rye,
Diddlediddle dumdum, Diddlediddle dumdum.
Sad to lose the old friends, say her eyes with a sigh.
About the funeral, do you hear me Mr. Bloom?
Did I tell you what Mr. Breen did, what he did last night?

Her hand, it rummages in her bag, her eyes fix on him.
What? Mr. Bloom asks rebounding to her world . . .
and on and on as a thought moves an image along,
now a sound to move a long lost memory,
and all of it chaotic for Mr. Bloom who feels
at times so real and at home on Dublin streets
but mostly is alone here as sounds and feelings
crowd in on him (so he won't feel so alone . . .)
and he is cold inside until a strong thought comes,
then for a single moment, Mr. Bloom is warmer,
before he's back on the train, our train of present to present.

PART SEVEN

while the French, Germans and Russians
care mostly how it acts . . .

THE UNREPENTANT VOLTAIRE

I'd see myself from this cliff on high,
that lipid, weak and shallow stream.
No pretense shows my discourse dry,
yet I'm not mordant as to wits I'd seem;
and defend myself against those vain ones
who've said I'm turbid, immoral, and weak,
that I've preferred mere facts over persons,
and missed the noble parts we seek.

Accused am I of destructive desires,
of building nothing of value or good
when seeking only what evil aspires,
and with the levity of the vain having stood,
morally blind to Godless possess
only a dark cavity in place of my heart,
one vile, profane, who'd with pen much address,
yet superficial and lacking all art.

From this Hell where I'm said to reside
I defend myself, my honor on earth,
and present *Candide*, these tales by my side.
Do they not equal Diderot's in worth?
Or Montesquieu's in wisdom and zest?
Can I not speak for my time as Rousseau?
Lo, you critics who claim all is best!
Did I not sing so your own words could flow?

GOETHE MEETING MEPHISTO AT LOW TIDE

Often I have fought the fierce storm and stress,
the chasm of a self unfulfilled
in places of seduction, sadness and death,
knew Western Man had struggled there,
unceasing in his foolish ways,
starving and hunting for Experience.

I found such a place out on mud flats
and met Mephisto at low tide waiting.
He offered an awful, cursed pact
and as the sea rose, foresaw my fate;
it was as the waves had long predicted,
what gulls had mocked and sang as I came:
my crimes would be by my Appetites caused,
yet the setting sun forgives such ways
and both good and evil stirred me to move.

Back in my village, fate waited for me
as I retold this short tragedy
by writing of my desperate brother Faust.

Forgetting Gretchen, all changed for him;
reborn, he breathed an intuitive joy.
It's through mirrored colors that we seize life,
he said as he began to live once more.
The truth he could at that time contemplate
for things such as this aren't known directly
but manifest themselves in reflections and signs;
and 'tis one thing to love another here,
yet beyond lies Spirit and Eros love.
So Faust left this world for clouds and ideals,
left Helen who, though not real, was true,
true as Plato's beauty or Apollo's.

Thus did Faust approach the emperor's court
and spoke in a subtle and noble tongue,
with a meter antique, perfect in every way.
She replied in her Germanic rhyme,
so joining Apollo and the German forms
and clasping upon his Nordic impulse
the elegance of graceful Greek ideals,
and a child was born this unified world.

Yet no fragile union will Nature hold
so Euphorion fell after scaling the cliffs,
and Helen followed his untimely death
when Faust was returned to this world of wills
and hoped for a height and felicity ahead,
making a vision both sad and sublime.
Mephisto, tracking his prey, seized this chance
and quickly moved in to devour us both
but we escaped in a triad of fate,
for the devil may have our active souls—
and perhaps the devil we always need—
yet he'll have only that same part of us
that to good and to heaven we have already given.

DOSTOEVSKY'S CORN OF WHEAT

Verily, verily, I say unto you, Except
a corn of wheat fall into the ground
and die, it abideth alone: but if it die—
truly die—it bringeth forth much fruit.

These words of Father Zosima were said,
   said to me as one of the murdering sons,
      but he could have said these words to all of us,
         to Dmitri whose suffering was by far the least,

or to Ivan who's not as yet here suffered,
   or to me, the lone and unconfessed Alyosha;
      for each of us should know that truth of life:
         that our hearts are but the torrid battlegrounds

wherein each day God and the devil fight,
   and that God gives to us a freedom to fight this war
      from which we are led to suffer and to fail,
         yet from this spiritual death comes rebirth.

Before God silent, unmoving we stand,
   each to fall, each to be reborn in Him.
      God, creator of light, cares not of night
         and allows us to suffer, then to live,

to love the family of men in which
   we all will live responsible for all
      and as our minds doubt so much, even God,
         as our reason shows him not to exist,

Father Zosima's art will this defeat.
    By him, I recall wheat falls to the ground
        and is thus reborn when under the sun.
            By him I know our souls fall as they must,

but with love will as spirits rise again
    and once more live as brothers and as sons.

THE TEMPTATIONS OF TOLSTOY

Long I struggled to be free in spirit and mind,
struggled to begin, my tale of adultery to find
demons and truths as words and lovers show.
So Anna was to be unredeemable and low,
fat to the point of disfigurement and profane,
while her cheated husband was higher and more urbane.
Yet as I wrote, Anna's life-like figure arose,
shedding her dress and donning Shakespeare's fatal clothes,
vibrant, alluring, worthy of my sympathy,
while Vronsky was cold, lost and past all empathy.
In my heart, Anna was the closest and most real;
to my touch, her fond Levin did most like me feel.

With angry cries and childhood ways they led me,
showing how women vexed and men tortured can be
and as they all exposed to me their graven features,
I saw myself as a student, saw them as teachers.
Anna, who fell from mid rank to lowest and worst,
became a woman of the streets and ever cursed,
leaving safety to be caught in passion's deep traps.
She told me the body and mind will never collapse,
that she knew by her choice from God she'd be severed,
yet it was by sensual love that she endeavored.
And Levin, by his choice of dark path and wan way,
showed me my own quest for faith in each darkened day;
estranged from God and driven his own life to take,
he yet found a faith his soul itself could then make
and in marriage to Kitty could still be fulfilled.
I wrote, *what he saw then, he never saw again*,
for he was moved by those riches God gives to men.
And there I was as there I am with this Levin,
walking between my lowly life and that far Heaven.

PART EIGHT

and the Americans claim to feel it where an *I* meets an *It*.

MELVILLE MEETING AHAB

When Ahab met me it was eighteen forty one
  and our jibs were luffing as the seas spoke of his timeless foe,
    a great whale, a white ghost, that he'd fought by tragic run.
      He told me and begged me—though buried so low—
        that he'd been, as we'd been, so selfish all this way,
      and lonely and cut off from the outer saving realm
    while searching and yearning a distant moral bay,
  that the hero is tragic who steers by the human helm.
For Ahab who met me was buried in the sea
  and eerie his low tone, that captain long since lost.
    His regret, his great flaw, what he showed so humanly,
      was the pride and the price that is our mortal cost.
      For Ahab loved water long before he was drowned
    and yearning the beyond as all voyagers do,
  saw the wind and the sea that tossed his vessel round
when he faced with his soul the white whale two and two,
and Ahab spoke sacred, said to me and ghostly pled,
  that whiteness and whale shapes we all will someday know
    where beauty is horror and colorless our minds are fed,
      where we sail on a sea made restless when our gods let us go.
      And lastly he told me in a watery, subtle tone
    that he'd found what we sought, something worth our quest,
  deserving of worship, not that power's moan,
but our own defiance, our truest voyage test.

EMERSON TO THE KILLER
AND THE KILLED

Do not gloat as you are killing men
and fear not you who would be killed,
for you cannot see my secret den,
this place your lives each day have filled.

Still, my visage your mind would frame
if you could think of one to whom
suns and shadows are but the same
and time of birth is night of tomb.

I, before whom all words fail,
will be your being, be your bliss;
and in me finite forms all fail
as karma earthen senses miss.

Heed these simple words to you:
as doubters all will see my way,
as lesser gods shall find me too,
when they to silent things will pray.

THOREAU IN HIS MANSION

Deep here within this fraternal wood,
primeval, untamed and of this earth,
I ask the red elders—never understood—
standing by their brethren white pine of worth,
why they called me here those two years past
and hearing nothing, move on to the wise spruce,
perfect in their form yet remaining masked
so that only their silences are let loose.
Still, I seek their words of a kinship true
and hope to learn what they know, what man once knew.

From the light green lichen on a nearby stone,
handsome, dappled with the shadows of those trees,
I hear faint songs in a language unknown
and touch a Grecian boulder's mossy frieze.
It acquaints me with vast, conspicuous masses
in my midst and ancient vestiges here,
the abundance through which nature passes,
makers of deep woodland sounds far and near;
and from this I recall I once sought to know
what's essential to life and from it to grow.

On that first spring morn, a mansion I entered
when in pre-dawn I sought nature alone
and heard not woods in which I was centered,
but voices through which they were outward shown.
It was my vague intent to sing anew
of nature, of life, of rewards pure and bare,
caring not of clothes, false skins or their rew,
for my hope was to see things high and rare.
Far from men and machinery so stalled,
I imagined life when in caves men crawled,

so this race who lived out of doors I found
as I shed all but what our basic needs give;
though alone I was warmed by the sun and the ground
when soon I sought shelter and ways to live.
In those first days, I gazed back upon friends,
seeing the formulae of time they used—
of property, government, pay for ends,
and I said just as Chapman once had mused:
we've false society our greatness made,
are poor while in luxuries we could wade.

Safe from the comforts of modern hands,
I sojourned in woods by Walden's Pond,
then sought to build a cabin on those lands
when I by my industry felt nature respond.
Fresh timbers I hewed to a shelter make,
racing the vaulting winter, toiled each day
to light fires within and warmth partake
and rest when cheeping squirrels' would say.
Then that harvest of beans grown in my field
a joy provided that no wealth could yield.

I've learned survival's no problem for most
if they'd live simply, wisely and well,
and seen philanthropy's no ground to boast
for those who'd seek what Heaven can't sell.
These two years later, by the red elders taught,
having lived out here my deliberate way,
the essence of life I had truly sought
but my own self I found each night and day,—
and now can say: to man's home I was led
when from nature, that knowing book I read.

WHITMAN'S LIFELONG DECLARATION

1

I declare myself that voice *The Poet* calls,
serve forth this as that ocular mound of words it predicts.

I follow not meter nor rhyme but announce my own form,
make meaning upon those things genuine, solid and real.

I speak to the farmer, the Indian, the child,
and guess not at them as they guess not upon me.
What I am, they are, for we are born of one human timber.

All those European paths that divide, I curse them
and place them into the melting sounds of my own voice.
All things elaborate, obtuse, arcane
are nothing to me, for I cannot use them to speak.

2

I touch the skin of the passerby and am mad to feel it again,
breathe the atmosphere of American trees and let it fill my lungs,
recall the poetic trilling of Romantic English fathers
      and use it for a more direct poem.
The pauses in my voice, the crackling noise, its hoarseness,
these things as well I use, combining them into my living words.

3

All things form originally at my feet and ask me to
      practice their ways.
Images are as sentences to me, asserting green shouts,
      yellow regrets.
Nothing is odorless or tasteless as no moment is timeless;
I feel my own health as the sun feels my perspiring brow.

The echo of a being is its voice, its movement, its verbal answers
    to the multitudinous soundings of nature.
I smell the salt in this shore before me and let it
    expand the moment, let it ripple throughout me now.

Searching inward, I hear the beating of my heart
    and am glad for it, eternally glad.

4

And who are you who I call out to in these fits and screams?
Are you alive as well, hearing me not in a poem,
    but as a thing held out to you by the earth?

How have you embraced this world my silent listener?
Will your soul, your American soul and bones, shed all
    haughty falseness?
Dismissing your deceptions, will you learn the sound of your
    own voice before it dies?

Henceforth I will welcome all into my earthen response to life,
bring in art, make it divide my soul,
welcome music so fully that it takes on the
    hue of humble happiness,
require my philosophy to work in my world, demand that it
    have a useable, every day meaning.

5

And where do you stand before me?
Do you urge Heaven toward us through your laughter
    or with your eyes?
Have you laid yourself crying before every stone that has
    beaten you and felt how its shape conforms to your heart?

Do you believe yourself to be seen and unseen at once,
    moving and still?
Can you sing your poems, read aloud your books, laugh loudly?

Who are you standing before me?

I announce the equanimity of all our souls, call you out
        from the road where you stand, place us into one.

6

All things pinch inward upon themselves in time
        and space and in every way.
We force them back through memory and longing and
        diverse translations of the moment,
through sex and outrage alike, we force them back.

I look upon this stone wall before me, set upon
        sand in a seaside night,
and I see a light shimmer upon it.
I choose to pull every shard of that light within,
for no one sees these stones and light,
        feels them as I do now.

My mind knows light and sound and touch as outward realms,
        but they are pulled into me by my will;
they are made inward objects, parts of my daily being,
        glowing and sounding and feeling within;
they are senses through which I am caressed by an inner world.

No moment is fused to another in time until I make it so,
        apply its meaning, give it a marking and name.
No sensation is everlasting, yet each surges toward death and
        bursts with a human gladness as if it is.

7

Hear me you breakers, you dispellers, you crucifiers in all
        times leading to my own;
hear me agents of hatred in my own time, in my very midst:
I end you, end you by the glare and the strength and the soundings
        of my focused mind.

You too who defile life, dispose of it as useless, who have ever
       been so rude to the invitations of life before you:
I use you as well to build my human voice, make you a part of me.
You too I take with me throbbing, pulsing, holding clouds
       as they pull me into eternity, that nightly, unfeeling and
       perfect human bliss.

ELIOT'S INVITATION

Might we now walk together out here, just you with me,
walk in this night of ours, our mutual eternity,
as we would if we were once again willing and able?
Might we, although this woodland path is not the same,
lacking the sounds we heard, the sounds of the living frame?
There! I was sure I just heard it, a squirrel's retreat,
but I couldn't have heard it and the ferns never moved by its feet.
Look up! See that? What is that there above us hovering?
It seems as if phantoms here are us discovering.
And didn't those stars just ask us, ask our secret question?
Just move on, you must never ever speak to them.
Might we just walk, walk in this forest a fate to stem?

This cabin dark and damp that we are walking in
reveals that here there was committed some great, eternal sin.
I can feel it . . . can't you feel it, right here beside the door?
See the blood calling to its host, the hair laying on the floor?
The air I breathe is much the same as it was that evening;
it floats about and moves in the rooms to us implore
and it lingers about the window-pane and silently escapes.
Let's follow it as it slips around the fallen tree;
let's see it avoid us till we exchange its secret for ours,
though now it glides over the pond to the places we cannot see.

But there is no longer a need for us to chase that air
for we, you and me, now have a lifetime to make it tame,
a lifetime to examine even the floor beside the door,
to breathe the outer fog and breathe the inner air,
and we will have a lifetime to hear it, hear it exclaim,
to find it by the window-pane poised in its stations;
there will be time for me to follow as you walk free,
time for a million of those mysterious revelations,
time for a million of our secrets and all those invitations,
and do not worry, we always will walk, just you with me,
unless this place so dark that we are walking in,
has somehow seen our last, our great, eternal sin.

THE PHILOSOPHERS

PART ONE

Listen to the philosophers, to the Greeks, who claim
there is but one soul . . .

THE TRUTH OF DEMOCRITUS

It was only after I
stepped out onto this road,
after I glanced down
at the pebbles of this modern road,
that I realized my prior self,
someone not a Tennessee

farmer at all, someone else,
and mumbled my prior name,
Democritus! and the images
of my youth returned,
the olive trees, the hills
with rocks, the busy city

of walkers and merchants;
and then I knew
what I had seen there.
The world was so large
and I felt desires
swell within me for

the kingdoms of Persia,
for knowledge of the cosmos,
but with this same immediacy,
I sensed the desires of an
older man who—
I now surely recall—

would rather discover
one cause, just one,
than those kingdoms
of Persia have won,
who believed that to chase
life's purpose is an idle race

if all nature is made
of atoms and space,
who said that by
indivisible things all
earth is done and,
once congregated,

all mass is thus begun.
It seemed this former
self once saw those atoms
as indestructible
and un-fated,
a free reality.

I, this ancient Greek,
cursed the lies
of Parmenides,
a sage who claimed all
was a continuum,
and not my entities.

To be a farmer
is to connect
every day to the
earth, the soil,
the weather and
non-human life,

and it is to
be content not
to prove anything
or advance thought
for future generations,
but to hold the land.

What, I wondered,
had this former
self proven?
And then I
recalled it,
the smaller truth:

that all this vast
realm is change,
that each thing
is made from
something before it,
something once proud,

that infinity is
made of little pieces
—as I saw the crops move
with the wind—and that
this self will die,
to prove my finitude.

PLATO AND THE COLORLESS HILL

My teacher to his student wisely asked
when he queried, *What is beauty if left unmasked?*
He asked not of things that beauty would gently adorn,
but of beauty herself, who lives through things forborne.
Justice he knew is not an act in time;
it rides through ages over man with forms in rhyme.
All things are fleeting to eyes, but deep is the soul
and deeper still its timeless essence toll.
A decaying fruit in life by time exists,
but its form endures and to worms of time resists.

Those who are from this light of truth now hid,
who from the cloak of darkness can't be rid,
still know the things they once perceived as real
did a harmony, an order and a measure to them reveal.
The number calls this truth through its nature and ways;
it fits in the realm of its kind and lives no days.
This wisdom great Pythagoras yearned to show
as he traced an unearthly path not of things that grow.
Perfection we see, ideas in locking rings,
when we soar to grasp the essential nature of things.

What rich and verdant green is that colorless hill
when the mind made blind is freed of hue and fill.
So let those senses not become your thoughts my men;
trust them not beyond their earthly ken,
for I watched the nymph of mind cast away her dress
and followed her road of everlastingness.
My passions steered no more as high I drove
past objects separate, sight, and fondest Jove,
to see a vast and formless castle appear,

and my mind recoiled as time began to steer.
I learned that things un-seeable are never seen,
that no tainted mind could capture a thing so clean.

ARISTOTLE AND THE NATURE OF BEING

Take Plato but truth is dearer still;
follow him, the realms he'd fill,
those ideas that cannot be seen,
that elude my substance of the mean.
Though worlds of wonder here will lie,
yet no less real do they belie;
for to know a thing and sense it through
requires quality, quantity too.
What is being? Plato asked;
it's substance when it has been unmasked.

O, the mind is deep, you say,
but look upon this very day
as every motion you should see,
each one formed by the same decree:
action will a becoming show,
as light makes colors ever glow,
our thoughts alter things we know;
to change all flow, from change you grow.
Purpose is form though not yet born,
as each tree causes its own acorn.

No number could ever exist
apart from the things that it would list.
It is numbers that are the things unreal,
for they need substance, its steady keel.
While my mentor two worlds once could see,
I to one, this world will be.
Though to him its not one real at all
and he would hear a timeless call,
I can't sense his abstract realm
in this moment real as acorn to elm.

EPICURUS, WHO WOULD COMFORT US

Listen to me, hear me verily:
you feel fears, burdens heavily,
yet for all these I speak to you;
answers to each given true.
From shackles I shall liberate,
live what I say and be free from hate.

First death, profoundest of all your demons,
the reaper of men and killer of seasons.
What do you fear? I ask you now,
when *nothing's there* aft life's plow.
Death would be yet nothing to you,
for when it arrives you are through.

Next God, his judgment stern below.
Condemned you believe, damned you know;
while this God, if he does exist,
dwells far away, deep in some mist.
cares not for *you*, to bless or damn,
is kin to rocks but not to man.

Pain, suffering, evil they make,
you want respite from them, joy in their wake.
I deliver you now from this thing,
most vexing thing which writhes to sing:
only a coward would flee from pleasure,
a potion *you* make to pain endure.

Last remorse and regret, two twins
who crouch in each of life's small wins.
Look forward and follow our vaulting time,
when never to the past does the present climb,
so for many a life some good may do
that soul once lost on a past untrue.

PART TWO

and the Christians who say this one soul is the
soul of God . . .

THE GREETING OF SAINT AUGUSTINE

Welcome you soul
   to this city, the city of God.
      Look around,
         be humbled as infinity you trod;

this place He's made
   for those whom He'd select,
      and now two worlds
         your eyes and mind erect.

We each have stood
   at the gates of two vast empires,
      and to heaven belongs
         as to hell for you transpires.

And now the truth:
   that all in heaven we know
      when bound for hell
         forever whence we go,

when no sinner has been
   saved nor ever will be
      and we are predestined
         for heaven or devilry.

Don't dread this fate,
   you not to masses born,
      see Plato's city,
         see its resplendent form,

recall the ocean,
    its flow then look to this place,
        how nature's earth and
            way are but a trace,

a hint of this,
    this city mighty and true,
        made not by man
            but toward a purpose new.

Trust not in reason
    but by your faith be led,
        free will by grace,
            the path that you have tread;

this city of time,
    this place beyond your terror,
        your will He knew
            this God who's free of error.

SAINT THOMAS AQUINAS
IN TRIBUTE TO ARISTOTLE

Good Aristotle, how you better knew
the way of God, his every earthly clue.
To see God's mind mere faith is but one code;
reason proves faith as Plato's student showed.

Though revelation be the better way
and those who use it have their lives today,
nature's things are as God will cause or draw,
and have the order of His divine law.

Thus, for a thinking few is unfurled
the way of reason to understand God's world.
Through either path we must will His bless'd end;
still to free will our lesser goals do bend.

Minds like *tabula rasa* all begin;
all that's now found there our senses did win.
Knowledge and revelation meet as one
for all the world is God's creation.

So God is apprehended to my mind
not as Anselm's speech on essence would find
but as understanding commends to me,
that the first and unmoved mover must be.

DUNS SCOTUS UPON THE
EVENT OF HIS DYING

In this moment, in the year thirteen o eight of our Lord,
I've passed from life and now to my maker have soared.
Just moments ago, reader, you'd have known me as living
but now I dwell in a world past nature's great giving,
so with strong conviction I may here argue and say:
be not by Aristotle or Aquinas led astray.

From this promontory I look upon thought anew
as a great ship with gaping holes and a fated crew
that failed as built upon two designs, one false one true,
sunken by life then strewn upon rocks as time will do.
Now seen through the specter of eternity, reason falls,
and sinks sadly beside the bark of faith with mighty walls.

This reason repels nature's waves and all that God has wrought
so you in life must now dissect what Aquinas thought.
Tend as I did not to reason's way but to faith's slow roll,
my mind thus found no proof of any immortal soul;
yet here I stand, in a place of which my faith would sing,
an eternal being, a soul that flies on a timeless wing.

PASCAL'S REASONS OF THE HEART

The heart after all has reasons that reason
does not know at all nor ever will.
To me a Jesuit hate is now drawn,
though I'm the traveler, they the lawn,
and great truths like flax your mind I'll fill.

I once was taken by reason's stare
and saw false prophets in logic's claim.
Hell's temptress sent me what brains ensnare,
took me to an absence I could not bear,
and still this false God I saw and could tame.

Life's wager then showed the truth to me,
that through faith nature never lied.
If I believe and yet God will not be,
then in death no harm shall come to me,
but wrongly deny and all Hell's astride.

This I know shall forever survive
and while it always the brain will repel,
in the heart this truth will ever thrive
while the heart's reasons will always strive
as no reason knows nor ever will.

PART THREE

but do not ignore those who speak of
our empirical selves . . .

BACON FALLEN

My life, the stature, all the fame I knew
when rising to be Lord and Chancellor,
now end as all my honored days are through;
at sixty I see a life that's imbued
with bribery, disgrace and shown the door.

Alone and poor, no power retained,
I'm left alone with memory and pen;
and yet my philosophy remains unstained
for thought civilized it now has gained,
and my tribute's this, not the office of men.

I believe I was near the first who saw
that science could be used for endeavors human.
And those like Descartes who spider webs draw
show us only the mind and its flaw,
that the outer world is truth's real ken.

Also, the empiricist I would condemn.
An ant and not a spider he has been,
hording facts but never using them.
But my way gives a *method* and a system
so knowledge begets a knowledge again.

And I would say our human interactions
display to us idols of tendency
within the marketplace we call our actions,
and words give us only our false reactions,
things I'd not confuse with reality.

HOBBES AND THE WORTH OF MAN

I know this true, that the worth of man
as of all things is but his price.
Thus, in these last counted moments I stand
and measure my life, the works of my hand,
to wander and count this life now thrice:

First, there's that thing that by me was said,
that matter exists and ideas do not,
that incorporeal substance is dead.
This the scholars of God and man have read
and to me assigned this curs'ed lot.

Second, there's my view of the human mind,
that only by physics could it be run,
that ideas lurk not a brain behind,
that matter shows all, not to vapor find
as all by one world, not two, is done.

Third, that the nature of man and state
is rules, the means for state controls.
Through fear of death we will create
our nature, self-interest and our hate
to thwart life's nasty and brutish tolls.

Last, for these views they've hated me,
but I've been free and rich till old age,
and when I'm asked, *How could it be?*
I answer, *dear critics, don't you see?*
You've asked what's only for our Sage.

THE NATURE OF HUME

Being the last to
write of sense,
being the first to
qualify beauty and
mind

this way,
being one who
sees Berkeley
miss the mark,
planting ideas

as ghostly trees,
I am one
—perhaps the
last in my time—
to deny the self.

His *I*,
his sense-bundle,
is a modern
fiction for a rotting
modern mind.

A thing barer
is truer
as when *event*
replaces cause
and effect

and if you
ask what all
this doubting
may prove,
look at

yourself, free
of unfelt trees
and yearning
for forests
still.

—

ROUSSEAU'S SOCIAL CONTRACT

I have read
Hobbes and
cannot agree
with that evil
instinct he sees

as I was
born good,
and in deepest
nature am
something

noble.

It is
that gentile
society of
his that
corrupts me,

severs me,
makes me
forever
interrupted,
incomplete,

savage.

In his State,
I return
only part
way to my
true self

and there
mimic
some truer
instinct
in nature's

turn.

PART FOUR

or the rationalists who connect the soul
to the thoughts of God.

DESCARTES' DESK

Knowledge of this
world is gained by reason,
and what is simpler
is truer in math,
so by this a real
certainty I might infer

as this morning
here in my study,
I begin with
objects outside the mind
and wonder
if I can trust this

experience or its kind,
then realize I
cannot, for things
often do not
fit to such appearances
or follow those ways

as when I'm
certain of what
I have dreamed;
so then let me
assume that all I see
is only an evil

demon redeemed.
If all I observe is
infected with falsehood,
what, I wonder,
may I trust in
to know or be?

Yet malignant spirit,
you've hardly won!
Though doubt is my tool,
my most simple
rod, what it shows
as fact is not undone.

It proves this *I*,
a *cogito ergo sum*,
and by this
I know that
there *is* a world
and there *is* a perfect God.

SPINOZA AS HE POLISHES LENSES

Looking down to these lenses I polish,
I see secrets and inner sanctities.
This year I refused my prior wish
of philosophy professor as my niche,
and chose these eccentricities.

What do I see in glass you ask?
What worlds or truths are ground so fine—
from the Bible, or great math our task?
Or are these truths from a science cask?
All these are true and thus are mine,

as all is One and the One divine,
as God's in all, by these two ways known.
Yet this Descartes' worlds could never align,
for if distinct are matter and mind,
how could one the other move alone?

God is the cause of all things in Him,
of this Cartesian truth is devoid.
Immutable order now seen is dim
as thought and substance are of His whim,
and these lenses of God I can't avoid.

LOCKE AND THE VOICE OF NATURE

Listen as nature speaks to thee,
to the logic she'll deliver;
she begs you to run with reason free
as senses will endeavor.

Run, ever run, through brush and sea
to her method then discover
and this was all well known to me
as senses will endeavor.

Seek not the mansion of mind so stately
or what it may deliver;
so much you'd seek is past it truly,
as senses will endeavor.

By this bark I now search the sea
and the mind knows less than the river;
for this I through all the senses see,
as senses will endeavor.

Examine me, my ability
and mind's limits I'll infer,
then nature's part be shown to me,
as senses will endeavor.

Galileo made this decree
when the stars he looked over;
others could not in his way see,
as senses will endeavor.

When born our minds then blank must be,
their data spilling over;
still objects we'll not truly see,
as senses will endeavor.

Reality, thing strange to me,
that unknown lurking treasure,
is as this self and subject be,
as senses will endeavor.

Between these two lies a mystery:
as the world, the self would sever
what unknowns would my will set free,
as senses will endeavor?

PART FIVE

The geography of the soul is traced by
the paths of ideas . . .

KANT WALKING HIS DOG

This morning
I walk my little dog,
tomorrow the same,
and ask to see the
outer world, out
past this human fog.

I was once asleep
in a dogmatic slumber,
then Hume awakened me
and Konigsberg
was remade so
a new world I'd see.

Locke made it
first of sensation,
then Berkeley
turned out matter
and beyond him came
Leibniz, but Hume

was that high priest of
reality who directed
my mind through
the razor sharp
knife of skeptical
thought.

Take my dog,
innocent as can be:
I show her the way home
and her world has
an order, but
one guided by a leash.

My mind is
limited as is hers,
not by the outer
realms explored
but by what
each sense gives,

as the senses
show me
what my thoughts
will afford.
Some colors
I see though some

are unknown; and
the world that exists
is one, yet another
when perceived alone,
as distant orbits
my mind will run.

For now, as
I guide my
friend home,
her familiar
realm is as real
as mine

when lost
I roam
and there no
true ground
I feel, since
if not for

each odd mental
rhyme, each
category of thought
by all others
called space and
time, my world

would be chaos,
and this world
I'll not know
as mind adds
to its flow an
inner rhyme,

and this little
dog of mine
is led by a
leash this way
to find just the
reality I show.

HEGEL DOWN MOUNTAIN STREAMS

Time is a
tiny rivulet
that flows
to an ocean
and suggests
its own destiny,

just as the wave
tells me all
I need to know
when its crest
feigns eternity,
or its spray

makes reality.
Trace back
all time
this way through
finite things
and witness

the birth of *Being*,
that organic thing,
see what it clings to,
that self-inspired
thing we call
the material world.

In this way,
mountains indicate
an enduring truth,
their ancient
colors speak
to man and

their rocks are a
morality made uncouth,
as their mosses make
the human voice;
and all this is
mind, is reality,

is idea's den, first blunt
and expressed in a hardened
state, then evolved
to man's
light expression,
the animated *Geist;*

so that clouds
show the nature
of all things,
that all is not
object but a
process of change.

See this pebble
on the shore?
This is *Becoming,*
as clearly as
it ever may
be seen.

Self-awareness is the
dirge of the *Absolute*;
God, full knowledge,
and One-ness will emerge
from conflict as
into the ocean our
rivulet will flow.

SCHOPENHAUER AND THE STORM
OF THE WILL

Nature in turbulent, tempestuous motion;
semi-darkness through black thunder-clouds that threaten;
immense, bare, overhanging cliffs shut out our view
as rushing, foaming masses of water ensue.

This I hear from wails of wind sweeping through ravines
past me, clinging to hostile nature's ugly scenes.
Upon this I depend and my will it may break,
yet one hope in this affliction I may still take.

Art's contemplation, aesthetic and thus sublime,
by which I gaze through will, through space and time,
and comprehend, unshaken, unconcerned,
ideas that, in their objects, are my will interned.

These fonder melodies universally express
the inner story of will becoming self-conscious,
that secret, that real thing living, longing and suffering,
that ebb and flow of the human heart enjoying.

It's not Hegel but Kant, his strong mind that I address
and where he has ended, let me begin to caress
those supple hints of the mind, its lasting truth
and write the great mystery profound and so uncouth.

I begin in a darkened forest, home of the will,
and see Kant's first error standing before me, still;
see reality is more than any collection of things,
for in mind only by space and time number brings.

Next, beside me tortured, the music now wails,
singing, *by error you believe mind all things entails.*
Causality cannot relate such foreign kin—
all is one and motives mere causes from within.

Then, cascading in mystery, winds whisper to me:
*Kant said the real outer things we never can see,
but you are 'knowing self' and 'outer thing'*
and by this I find my path—not without but within!

High above the clouds, I find remorse
and retreat to what's felt as will, seen as force,
and there say, *you storm of death, my final call,
be my blind will, my dark and hallowed hall.*

FICHTE AND THE REJECTION OF KANT

When Kant spoke of starry
heavens above and
our moral laws within,
I wondered
why these two
worlds aren't closer,
asked which came first,
the mind or the outer
universe's state.

At first it was easy
to declare as my brethren did—
by the eyes of Locke,
the wit of Hume or
the nobility of scientists—
that the world causes the mind,
though we know not how;
but then I thought
perhaps nature
follows the mind.

I realized we make
laws and from them
deduce our observations
and reality by this is made,
bound in mind's
noose. Kant's laws, when
perceived as one,
are mere morality. My
willing self creates
its own realm in which to be.

So this world now teeming,
incredible and diverse,
my mind makes
before it in all its fields;
I know myself
not as a thinking
but a moral state,
for when I act
I choose and the moral
world I thus create.

SCHELLING AND THE RISE OF BEING

Imagine if you can, imagine,
   a great being sleeping, restless and still;
    believe in your mind, merely believe,
     that she grew and breathed.

Name her simply, please help me name her.
   Is it *Nature*, this name that you have chosen?
    Pity you say, such pity you find,
     that one so elegant could be born blind;

yet look now, look and you shall see,
   observe her fecundity and her form;
    she's grown a feature called *man* so fair,
     an eye to see so she's self-aware,

and recall that Fichte called her dead matter
   with Nature a creation of the self;
    then declare, declare the opposite true,
     that Nature, our great unity, made mind anew

and you'll see her living, see evolving Nature,
   you'll know that we're mere spiritualized matter.
    Yet still a question will this enthrall:
     Why does she exist? Why her at all?

ROYCE'S ODE TO HEGEL

I have read the
physical geographies
of the sea
and a river runs
through the ocean
I have heard.

I have read Hegel,
felt his passion,
let his vision return
and the world
becoming is one
I have understood.

These complete
my lessons in a
single full turn.
To unite the
finite and infinite,
see the temporal

with the eternal
and the intimate,
this is my
idealist, my
modern, my
personal goal.

Pragmatists brought
me out from
the western
hills but their
cold view
of truth I

did not share.
It is not just
in spite of
this finite ride,
but *for it* that
in freedom
we reside.

Hegel is grand
yet can he be understood?
Man is finite so
God is omnipresent
and free;
I conceive human

limits in this way.
I suggest the
Absolute with
each breath and day,
and from imperfection,
we know perfection.

By a plan,
a purpose and its
fulfillment flow
so that partial things
imply the complete,
and in the unfulfilled

self a greater
community lies.
I listened once
to a lecture
by a mapper of
underground worlds.

He told me
that earth's
history is buried
beneath the sea.
I asked if
it is true that

a river runs
through the ocean
and he smiled
and he laughed,
then looked me
through and through.

For James and Peirce
error is possibility,
but for me
it is actuality
and we ourselves
show infinite unity.

By conscious thought,
God's great glory
is in me,
and reality
is the true
object of all ideas.

I see only
what seem to be
disconnected fragments,
for only God
is adequate and real and,
to be fulfilled, I must

feel the will
of others, just as
to know my earth
I must sense
a river in the ocean
and history in its sands.

PART SIX

and when described by the moderns it is the uniting of
the self with a transcendent realm.

WHITEHEAD'S POSTHUMOUS PLEA

Finally can we not announce that it is over?
    That the vast spinning of philosophical systems,
so intricate, self-proving and incomprehensible,
    based on some substance unknown is finally over?
Is it now not time to look honestly at modern thought
    with all of its philosophical confounding?
Can we not see Plato as greater still than Kant,
    as thinking more of organism than thought?

Will we not look back and see all philosophy
    as mere footnotes from Plato to salvage or delete
and realize the Copernican revolution
    was not any revolution for philosophy?
Can we not be frank my friends and recall
    all the great logicians, scientists and theologians
for a conversation to apprise their modes of thought
    and remind them of their purpose, make them recall?

Remind them that they were to *clarify* the universe
    and blame most the modern metaphysicians who stand
blithely by us refusing to tame speculation,
    make it coherent and make it *interpret* our universe.
If you will not announce it, then I will say it's over,
    and make a system rational and empirical
whose governing principle is one of organism,
    who'd describe the world as one, as coherent all over.

You ask what this organism does, how it is divided.
    As an ultimate, to exist, to explain and oblige.
This ultimate is creative as Plato's forms once showed
    and existence has eight birthmarks it shows through change.
Invert Spinoza and objects are not inferior;
    within the organism, real things are the ultimate,
they always perish yet flow in creative advance,
    for as in *Timaeus*, all is birth and change.

This flux, this flow, is greater than life and non-life,
    a process to include them both, subsuming man and God.
Thus God does not outside our world ever stand;
    He's a thing and not an occasion as we are in life.
Can we not step back in this way and finally find
    a metaphysics consistent with science and with our sense?
Can we not look out to this fluent and becoming world
    and through this pervasive feeling, our reality find?

NIETZSCHE AND THE MOUNTAIN HERMIT

Zarathustra, the mountain hermit
whom ten years of meditations fit,
with only his fond eagle of pride
and serpent of wisdom he'd confide.
Then, when he'd learned to think and know,
decided to teach the men below.

Along the way a saint would say
it was best to be alone and pray;
yet he refused, for man's alone
and can't expect to here atone
when God is dead in his wide world,
where man unmade hath God so hurled.

He found a town and crowd so awed
and told them man's profoundly flawed,
evolved from apes, still with their station,
fooled by those who'd promise salvation;
and no one listened, not a man—
they shunned him and his Overman.

What awed them was a circus performer,
an actor high, a tightrope walker.
But he fell and to the corpse was said,
I'll teach to man existence meaning—
the Overman, and the lightning beaming.
He set out then to find a flock,
those who'd all the others mock.

Anyone, the man went on to preach,
should be much more than he can reach,
and he's come alive the Overman
who lives and won't believe a man,
who'd easily achieve this state
by knowing not the mass's fate.

By this short tale I mean to say
that preaching in the conventional way
is fostering meekness and is corrupting
the will to power that is erupting,
and makes men nothing ever give
when lacking courage even to live.

These pitiful souls, these shepherded men,
escape to sleep and live again,
to favor the soul over the body,
seeking peace not war or folly.
What makes virtue in the Overman
is the freedom from God and a focus on man.

That release to the supposed afterlife
is an avoidance of our lifelong strife.
When asked what the Overman could reap,
answer joy and that life he'll keep.
He'll pass false belief and idle hope
to the power of his mind with which he'll cope.

SARTRE IN ECHOES

A cobalt sky was striated with bright sun beams
set out behind a cambric of clouds and dreams,
and nature's ample scene an anthem sang
of universal man just as his centrum rang,
but down from heavens, down to earth we'd see,
domains so crude of water, rock and tree.

Upon this place we found our artless friend
and watched him emerge from around a mountain bend.
His hike had ended upon our lofty grass,
he'd climbed life's hoary mountain, scaled its mass.
Monadnoc, Delphi, perhaps Mecca was its name
and at the peak he spoke these words of fame:

O being, what is your essence? Please tell me my fate.
And what is truth or meaning? For what do I wait?
Right as he posed these questions, shouting to the sky,
a hollow echo answered his desperate cry:
O being, what is your essence? Please tell me my fate.
And what is truth or meaning? For what do I wait?

He learned this then upon our mountain lawn—
that consciousness is emptiness though lonely, sad and wan,
that while he once believed the world first came
that all things are found by the mental frame,
yet his inner self chose but its own desire,
and his echo alone that truth he sought entire.

O being, what is man's essence? the philosophers ask.
He has none; existence precedes his every mask.
And what is his fate? He has none because he is free;
his future he forms himself creatively,
and meaning's what exigencies will make;
the truth is subjective, and all else we must forsake.

Our friend, once hearing the answers were but his own,
awaited replies, then found himself alone
and anxious of freedom, he faced his deepest fears,
of loneliness and Godlessness, the advance of death as it nears,
and felt so nauseous from the sound of his shattering dreams,
then thought he heard voices from the speech of mountain streams.

JAMES GRIEVING ON MONADNOC

I choose this day, in July of eighteen eighty five,
a place atop a mountain green—so full and alive—
to bury in a little hole my year-old son
and tell you now, my future friend, of your life's run.
Hear Mount Monadnoc, Emerson's proud sphinx so wise,
who'll swallow my young fighter, who'll this morning rise,
who knows you'll die and one more mind he'll then consume,
and some doubt his power but all will face his earthly tomb,

so dive this day—before you dwell within the earth—
into the stream of consciousness, thought's place of mirth,
and find there the tainted psychic fringes, the gravest sense,
move deep within that flow of thought's insouciance,
for all mind's images are steeped and dyed you see
in deep free waters flowing 'round them constantly.
They bring the sense of near and far, those subtle waves
of whence all comes, all things for which the body craves,

and seek not the image but what surrounds it in minds,
the halo that will escort it when a thought it finds,
that stately, spare companion once to the image fused;
see them apart as if to you they now have mused.
You'll doubt as I that this stream can reach ethereal realms,
you'll sense it though, its span, as you it overwhelms.
We know where we go—we're there right now in this grand flow:
it's truth we make through experience—to truth we go.

I see in the fate of my boy these strange and mystic waters;
he now receives a thing part ordered as mind infers,
yet part inherent pattern of a world beyond all mind,
a pre-existing place to him I pray is kind.
My little Herman, your struggling final days of sickness
were with your mother as was your birth, that loveliness.
To me, her goodness and your strength were lessons won
and then, flower of the human flock, you were undone.

At six o'clock this clear New Hampshire mountain morn
we left, Alice and I, by buggy out to mourn
as one, to gather pine and oak and young birch leaves,
those wild flowers, ferns and grasses remorse receives,
all to deck his little coffin as if rehearsed.
We found a wicker basket to make his cradle first,
then draped white canton flannel 'round his oak-wood bed
and laid him in with tree sprays 'round his little head.

We placed the flowers, ferns and grasses there at his feet
and with this lovely custom felt him then retreat.
There was some human need embodied there and so,
by the flow of this tradition, we felt him slowly go.
We looked at him as our desperate thoughts cut their deepest turns;
we spoke our prayers and saw the branches and the ferns,
then noticed how they bent o'er him to mark just when
the wicker lid had smothered him in his oak-fern den.

As horses drove us out we thought: there lies another,
one more lasting experience to bind us now together,
one more bitter taste of life's unbearable ways,
yet still, it shows the mysteriousness that before us lays,
that thing we call existence in the pragmatic sense,
unseen its realm past grief and every human tense.
O plural, restless universe, O mystic world,
O silent sphinx, accept this good that's now unfurled.

BUBER'S SACRED WORLD

I
and Thou,
this sacred relation here,
pervading every station's sphere,
Thou and
I

I
cannot
exist, though, independently
and must here in relation be
to an
It

I
as inner
require the world's broad outer sense
and act through life's experience
with an outer
It

One
last secret:
the I described by only It
is seen just as those parts would fit,
not whole as
One

Thou,
encountering
the I, reveals our nature, showing all,
and sings its eternal living call,
a love through
Thou.

TATE PUBLISHING, LLC

127 East Trade Center Terrace
Mustang, Oklahoma 73064

(888) 361 - 9473

TATE PUBLISHING, LLC
www.tatepublishing.com